THE ROYAL
HORTICULTURAL
SOCIETY

Fresh *from the* Garden

HENRIETTA GREEN

ILLUSTRATED BY SALLY MALTBY

KYLE CATHIE LIMITED

First published in Great Britain 1994 by
Kyle Cathie Limited
7/8 Hatherley Street
London SW1P 2QT

ISBN 185626 154 9

A Cataloguing in Publication record for this title is available from
the British Library

Designed by Lisa Steffens

Printed by The Bath Press, England.

CONTENTS

Introduction by Henrietta Green
Fresh From the Garden

One of the greatest pleasures in compiling *Fresh from the Garden* proved to be the cooking – I so enjoyed experimenting with the bounty of our native vegetables and fruits. All too often we discount our vegetables, considering them as no more than a mere accompaniment to the main course – a remnant of the British 'meat and two veg' philosophy. As for our fruit; in the rush to buy exotics imported from goodness knows where in the world, we are in serious danger of neglecting our own-grown varieties.

Personally I can never eat enough of either vegetables or fruit, whether raw or cooked, as a first or main or last course. Imagine my surprise when I recently read about a healthy eating project set up to encourage families to aim at five servings of them a day – some families were struggling to reach their quota. I assure you if it had been me, I would have thought five servings a serious deprivation, so important are they to my daily diet. And I can only urge you to eat as much of them as you can possibly manage. Not only are they versatile and truly glorious but also extremely good for you in providing a well balanced diet.

It is their amazing range of flavours, textures, shapes and colours that is so appealing. To cook without them would be like using a pen without ink – it doesn't work. When, sadly now several years ago, I had my own sunny vegetable patch in Gloucestershire, it was overgrown with just about every variety going. Imprisoned in a London flat now, I long for those days when I could rush out, basket in hand, and pick or dig up my daily needs. I have to make do – probably like the vast majority of us – with what I can buy or sometimes scrounge from generous friends with their own plots. But as a compensation for my long lost country days I visit many a farmshop or Pick-Your-Own. Generally they are a reliable source for super-fresh vegetables and fruit (that is when it is their own-grown rather than just bought-in stock) and if you are feeling lazy or pushed for time, you can often buy pre-picked.

In fact, almost everywhere, over the last few years the choice and freshness of fruit and vegetables on sale has vastly improved thanks, in no small way, to the supermarkets. I remember, years ago, searching fruitlessly for fresh garlic in Worcestershire; every greengrocer looked at me as if I were mad. Now you can find garlic in every corner of Britain with some of it even grown in here. When choosing vegetables or fruit, it goes without saying you should always buy them in as fresh a condition as possible. Droopy leaves, wrinkled skins, shrivelled fruits are the obvious tell-tale signs of old age so go for plump, pert specimens that look as if they have just been plucked from the fields. And never over-handle your vegetables or fruit; like us delicate humans, if you are too rough, they bruise easily.

Growing your own is a different matter. One piece of advice, given by a wise old farmer whose vegetables swept the board annually at our village show, was to 'go for the unusual. Why grow ordinary fruit or vegetables – the plain varieties,' he would ask? It makes sense; why indeed as although nothing beats produce straight from the garden, when it's in season in your garden so will it be in the shops. Far better to search through the catalogues for the varieties that offer the best flavour or unusual shapes or sizes or colour. And, unlike commercial growers, you are not governed by the considerations of consistency of size or large profit-making yields.

For the really 'unusual' I cannot recommend highly enough the Heritage Seed Library at Ryton Organic Gardens, Ryton on Dunsmore, Coventry, Warwickshire CV8 3LG tel 0203 303517. For a small subscription, you can join up and order seeds from old-fashioned and often endangered varieties that have great taste and flavour but are no longer considered commercially viable by the seedsmen.

Finally I must thank my trusted friend and fine cook in her own right Carla Capalba for all her hard work and help. Thanks too to Andy and Chris of my trusty London greengrocer Michanicou, in Notting Hill Gate, and to all the other cookery writers who have allowed me to plunder their ideas. They are too numerous to mention although I must single out Phillipa Davenport, Patricia Lousada and Marie-Pierre Moine.

So whatever you grow or buy, I hope you enjoy the recipes and that, like me, they will inspire you to broaden your fruit and vegetable cookery vocabulary.

SOUPS

PUMPKIN SOUP IN A PUMPKIN

Taken from Sophie Grigson's popular book, Eat Your Greens, this recipe for
pumpkin soup is served in the whole pumpkin once its flesh has been scooped out.
For the best possible effect, make sure you choose an evenly shaped,
unblemished specimen. Serves 4.

1 ripe pumpkin weighing
* 1.75-2.25kg/4-5lb*
15g/½oz butter
Salt and freshly ground
* black pepper*
55g/2oz long-grain rice
2 shallots, finely chopped
2 cloves garlic, peeled
* and finely chopped*

2 sprigs of fresh thyme
1 sprig of fresh rosemary
1tbs fresh parsley, finely chopped
575-700ml/1-1¼pt milk
30g/1oz Parmesan,
* freshly grated*
Crisp croutons to serve

1. Preheat the oven to 350°F/180°C/gas mark 4.

2. Using a sharp knife, cut out a lid off the pumpkin. Scrape out the seeds and
   threads and throw away. Rub the butter around the inside of the pumpkin and
   season generously with salt and pepper.

3. Put the rice, shallots and garlic in the pumpkin. Add the thyme, rosemary and
   parsley. Bring the milk to the boil and pour into the pumpkin to almost fill it.
   How much you use depends on the size of the pumpkin. Cover with its lid, wrap
   some foil loosely around it, taking care not to spill the contents, and stand in a
   roasting tin. Bake in the oven for about 1¾-2½ hours or until the flesh is tender.

4. Before serving, stir in the Parmesan and season to taste. To serve, scrape out
   some of the softened pumpkin flesh into each plate and ladle the soup on top;
   pass the croutons around separately.

A member of the Cucurbitaceae family with the cucumber, melon, vegetable marrow and summer and winter squash as close relations, the pumpkin is also known as a pompion or gourd. It comes in an extraordinary range of sizes and colours – from a creamy-white brushed with pale green, through yellow or ochre to an intense orange; but it has to be said all pumpkins taste virtually the same.

Its flesh is only mildly scented – the reason why the best recipes always contain strong flavoured ingredients – and considering how much water a pumpkin contains, is surprisingly solid. Favourite varieties are 'Hundredweight', an apt name for its huge size, and the more manageable, miniature 'Jack-be-Little'.

Grow a pumpkin as you would a marrow or squashes and should you want to, you can store it. It should be left on the plant to mature until the stems start to dry and the skins harden. A whole pumpkin will keep for months in relative humidity at a more or less constant temperature around 54°F (12°C). If buying one, remember to check for bruising.

OUILLADE

Almost a meal in itself, this is a hearty, robust soup.
For the best of all flavours and textures, I like to use a wrinkly-leaved Savoy
cabbage; failing that, a smooth-leaved, tightly-hearted winter cabbage
gives plenty of 'punch'.
One word of warning, taste the soup before you add the Roquefort
as it can be quite salty. For a gentler flavour, you might be better
off using a milder blue – like Danish or Shropshire. Serves 8.

2tbsp olive oil
2 large onions, chopped
2 carrots, sliced
2 celery sticks, sliced
1 turnip, sliced
4 garlic cloves, finely chopped
1 small hock of unsmoked bacon,
weighing about 900g/2lb
450g/1lb white haricot beans,
soaked overnight in water

1 small green cabbage,
finely sliced
3 'Wilja' or other boiling
potatoes, sliced
2tbsp fresh curly parsley,
finely chopped
freshly ground black pepper
55g/2oz Roquefort, or other blue
cheese (optional), crumbled

1. In a deep saucepan, heat the oil over medium heat and sauté one of the onions, the carrots, celery, turnip and two of the garlic cloves until soft. Add the bacon, brown for a couple of minutes, then add about 1l/1¾pt water or just enough to cover and bring to the boil over a medium heat. Cover and simmer for about 45 minutes.

2. Drain the beans and add to the saucepan. Add about 575ml/1pt of water and bring to the boil over a medium heat. Cover, simmer for about 35 minutes, or until the beans are tender.

3. Add the cabbage and potatoes and simmer for about 15 minutes, or until the vegetables are cooked.

4. Remove the hock from the pan. Once it is cool enough to handle, skin it, trim off the fat and chop the bacon into bite-sized chunks. Add these to the soup, then simmer for a further 5 minutes to reheat the beans and meat.

5. To finish, mix the remaining garlic and onion and the parsley together in a bowl and stir into the soup off the heat. Add plenty of black pepper and, if you think it can take it, the cheese, a little at a time, just to be on the safe side. Serve immediately.

PEA AND PEAR SOUP

Serves 4

A simple but effective recipe given by Sonia Stevenson of The Horn of Plenty fame to Lindsey Bareham for her excellent book *In Celebration of Soup*. In summer you can make it with fresh young peas and ripe pears, in winter it works with packets and tins instead. Either way the soup can be served hot or cold.

All you do is cook about 450g/1lb of fresh or frozen peas in salted water for a few minutes. Take about 800g/1¾lb very ripe pears or 2 x 400g/14oz tins unsweetened pears, drain the liquid from the cans into a measuring jug and make it up to 900ml/1½pts with cold water or you could use only water. Liquidize the pears with the peas and the liquid. Then pour the lot into a saucepan, add about 2 tablespoons of finely chopped fresh mint or the same amount of mint jelly and simmer until it is heated through. Season to taste with salt and freshly ground white pepper.

CHILLED
BROAD BEAN SOUP WITH SAVORY

Broad beans and summer savory are a cunning combination; it makes sense when you realise that they are in season in the garden at the same time. If you can, pick only the tiniest of broad beans with soft tender skins that 'melt' when cooking, then you will not even have to go to the trouble of passing them through a sieve. Serves 4.

700ml/1 ¼pt chicken stock
450g/1lb broad beans, shelled
1 tbsp summer savory, finely
  chopped and a few leaves
  for decoration

juice of ½ lemon
salt and freshly ground
  black pepper
3tbsp double cream
3tbsp plain yoghurt

1. Bring the stock to simmering point, add the broad beans, keeping aside about 4 whole ones.

2. Cook the beans gently for 5 minutes, drain and reserve the stock. Purée the beans in a vegetable mouli; if you do not have one, you can always use a food processor then pass them through a sieve afterwards to remove their skins.

3. Stir the purée into the stock, add the summer savory and the lemon juice. Adjust the seasoning.

4. Chill the soup for at least 3 hours. To serve, swirl in the cream and yoghurt, peel and chop the reserved broad beans and use them as decoration with the whole savory leaves.

POTATO, CUCUMBER, SALMON AND DILL SOUP

Choosing the right potato for the recipe in hand is not always easy. For this soup,
I like to use a variety that, while floury and soft after cooking, will not dissolve
into a purée. 'King Edwards' and 'Maris Piper' fit the bill. Serves 4-6.

800g/1 ¾lb cucumber, peeled
45g/1 ½oz butter
4 spring onions, finely chopped
225g/8oz potatoes,
   peeled and cubed
1l/1 ¾pt vegetable or fish stock

3tbsp fresh dill, chopped
salt and black pepper
250ml/8fl oz sour cream
75g/3oz smoked salmon,
   cut into thin strips
sprigs of fresh dill, to garnish

1. Cut the cucumbers in half lengthwise and scoop out the seeds and discard. Chop the cucumbers finely.

2. Heat the butter in a pan and sauté the spring onions with the cucumbers for a few minutes. Add the potatoes and stock to the pan and bring to the boil. Stir in the dill, lower the heat and simmer for about 15 minutes or until the vegetables are soft. Adjust the seasoning, remove from the heat and stir in half of the sour cream.

3. To serve, ladle the soup into individual serving bowls. Spoon a dollop of the remaining sour cream in the centre, and scatter over the smoked salmon and sprigs of dill. If you prefer to serve the soup cold, chill it for at least 3 hours, then stir in half of the sour cream and proceed as above.

STARTERS

FRIED COURGETTE FLOWERS STUFFED WITH RICOTTA AND BASIL

In most Mediterranean markets at the height of summer, you are certain to stumble over baskets piled high with freshly picked, golden-yellow courgette flowers. Whether from the female courgettes en fleur or attached to taut male stems that, as every frustrated gardener knows, will never swell up and fruit, they are a joy to eat.

SERVES 4

12 male courgette flowers

Batter
85g/3oz flour
250ml/8fl oz water

Tomato Sauce
4tbsp olive oil
1 medium onion, finely minced
1 clove of garlic, chopped
450g/1lb tomatoes, chopped
pinch of sugar

small bunch of basil
salt and freshly ground
  black pepper

Stuffing
200g/7oz fresh ricotta cheese
1 egg
2tsp fresh chopped basil
salt and freshly ground
  black pepper
olive oil for frying

1. Make the batter by beating the flour with the water in a bowl. It should be the consistency of double cream but if it is too thick, just add a little more water. Cover and set aside to rest.

2. Meanwhile prepare the tomato sauce by heating the oil. Add the onion and sauté for about 5 minutes or until golden brown. Stir in the garlic, tomatoes, sugar, basil and a couple of tablespoons of water. Season and simmer gently for about 20 minutes. Finally purée in a food processor until smooth.

3. Prepare the flowers by removing the pistils from inside the flowers and clean them by carefully rinsing the flowers in cool water or wiping them with a damp cloth. Gently shake or pat them dry.

4. Prepare the stuffing in a mixing bowl by whipping the ricotta until smooth. Beat in the egg, basil and season with salt and pepper.

5. Fill each flower with a couple of tablespoons of the stuffing, taking care that the flowers are only about two-thirds full. (If you over-fill them, they may burst while cooking.) In a suitable pan, pour in the oil to about the depth of 2cm/¾inch and heat to hot but not smoking. Dip the flowers into the batter, drain slightly and fry, a couple at a time, turning, until golden. The trick is to fry in small batches so the pan is never over-crowded. Using a slotted spoon, remove the flowers from the pan and drain on paper towels. Serve immediately with the fresh tomato sauce.

Courgettes – or zucchini as they are known both in Italy and in the States – are really baby marrows. But what a difference they offer in flavour and texture – soft, succulent, with a velvety finish. They are a glorious addition to our vegetable treasury.

Now you can grow or buy them bell-shaped (ideal for hollowing out, stuffing with rice then roasting) and the palest of pale green or bright cheery yellow as well as the ordinary straight fingered bottle green. Remember that the longer you leave the fruit on the plant, the fewer female flowers will grow and the more the later crop will be reduced.

At their best courgettes should be eaten when as small as a baby finger and certainly when no bigger than about 22.5cm/9inches long. Anything larger than that and they will have lost their natural intensity, their gentle grassiness coupled with a vital hint of sweetness.

As with all vegetables, it is a question of age and size; large courgettes can be quite bitter or watery and their skin is almost certain to be tough. A good test for freshness as well as age is to run your fingernail along its side. If the skin wrinkles it is past its prime.

STEWED ARTICHOKES WITH HAM AND PEAS

*Although most cooks regard globe artichokes as a foreign vegetable,
they were extremely popular with the Victorians, even served at their shooting
parties. This recipe is particularly useful at pruning time, it is an ideal way of
using the lateral artichoke buds, those small heads that are so tender you can eat
them whole without any fiddly preparation. Serves 6.*

juice of ½ lemon	*150ml/¼pt dry white wine*
4 large or 12 small artichokes	*115g/4oz fresh shelled peas*
4tbsp olive oil	*small bunch of mint, chopped*
2 garlic cloves	*salt and freshly ground*
75g/3oz prosciutto, diced	*black pepper*

1. Mix the lemon juice into a bowl of water and put in the prepared artichoke segments to soak when they are ready, to prevent discolouring. Prepare the artichokes one at a time by trimming off the tip of the stem with a sharp knife, then peeling it to get rid of any coarse, stringy fibres. Pull off the small leaves around its base and carry on pulling off the tough outside leaves, working towards the centre. Trim the artichokes by cutting off the top of the leaves, either with a sharp knife or a pair of scissors. Cut the artichoke into 4 or 6 segments, right through the heart and leaves, and scoop out the choke from each segment.

2. Drain the artichoke segments and pat them dry with paper towels. Heat the oil in a saucepan, add the garlic and prosciutto and sauté for a couple of minutes. Then add the artichokes, stirring to coat them thoroughly with the oil. After a further 3-4 minutes pour in the wine, turn up the heat and let it bubble for another couple of minutes.

3. Stir in the peas and mint and season to taste. Turn down the heat to a gentle simmer, cover the pan and leave the artichokes to cook until tender when pierced with the point of a knife. Depending on their size it should take between 25 and 35 minutes. Serve immediately.

BRUSCHETTA

Serves 4

There are any number of combinations of ingredients that can be used for a bruschetta. Italians might argue that the 'real thing' has to have tomatoes – but who needs such purists?

The main thing is to start with a really good bread – preferably made with olive oil like ciabbata – then cut it into thinnish slices and grill it on both sides until it is a honey brown. While the toast is still hot, rub a peeled raw garlic clove against one side, as you would against a grater, and – believe it or not – it has exactly the same effect. Then you need to dribble some olive oil on top – and the better the quality of olive oil, the better the taste of the bruschetta, so go for an extra virgin olive oil.

Finally comes the topping. And here you really let your imagination run riot. How about a few roughly chopped, very ripe tomatoes mixed with a few slices of crumbled goat's cheese; or a handful of chopped mixed herbs – coriander, flat leaf parsley, thyme, rosemary or oregano – mixed with a couple of chopped black olives and moistened with a little extra olive oil? Another favourite is chopped cucumber, avocado and spring onion tossed in Three Pepper Oil (see page 24); grated courgettes (just use the grating disc on the food processor) mixed with olive oil, a dash of lemon juice, some chopped tarragon and lashings of black pepper always goes down a treat.

GRILLED VEGETABLES
WITH THREE PEPPER OIL

*As well as the vegetables suggested below, you can also grill leeks,
fennel, even corn on the cob. And if you have got a barbecue going outside, use it
instead. Just prepare the vegetables as suggested, then put them
on a lightly oiled rack about 15cm/6inches from the glowing coals,
remembering to turn and baste them occasionally. Serves 4.*

For the oil
8-10 black peppercorns,
   lightly crushed
8-10 white peppercorns,
   lightly crushed
8-10 pink peppercorns,
   lightly crushed
300ml/½pt extra virgin
   olive oil

1 firm medium aubergine
2 medium courgettes
2 yellow or red peppers
1 red onion
4 medium flat mushroom caps
sea salt

1. To make the Three Pepper Oil, simply mix the peppercorns in with the oil and
   leave it to stand for at least a couple of hours. Remember the longer the oil is
   left to infuse, the more fiery it will be. It could stay stoppered in a bottle for
   weeks.

2. To prepare the vegetables, slice the aubergine into 1cm/½in thick rounds and
   cut the courgettes lengthwise into ½cm/¼in slices. Quarter the peppers,
   discarding the inner seeds. Peel and cut the onion into quarters; and if you leave
   as much as possible of the pale root section at the top, this will stop the onion
   from falling apart on the grill. Wipe the mushrooms with a damp cloth.

3. Preheat the grill. Using a pastry brush, paint the vegetable pieces all over with
   the flavoured oil. Arrange them on the grill pan in a single layer, and grill,
   turning and basting occasionally with the oil if they start to dry out. Cooking
   times will vary according to the heat of the grill, how near you place the grill
   pan and the thickness of the vegetables; but you should allow about 10-15
   minutes. To see whether they are done, test by piercing with the point of a

sharp knife. When the vegetables are tender, they are ready to eat. Sprinkle with sea salt just before serving.

Surely one of the greatest pleasures for a cook/gardener is to tend a herb garden? Your own patch, whether it's a formally laid out plot or no more than a few pots on a window sill, can supply the kitchen with great delights and every serious cook will always tell you that nothing, absolutely nothing, replaces fresh herbs when cooking.

Amongst my favourites are Moroccan mint (during the summer I crush the leaves for a refreshing tea) or lemon thyme with its citrusy sharpness for adding to chicken. Feathery chervil, with its merest hint of aniseed, goes literally in handfuls into many a salad, while salad burnet lends a cucumber-cool flavour. Sweet cicely cuts the sharpness when stewing rhubarb whereas a few sorrel leaves will sharpen any sauce.

All edible flowers are welcome in my herb garden. Hyssop's blue or pink flowers or the brightest of bright blue tiny borage flowers can be scattered on top of lettuces as can heartsease or the petals of pot marigold. Gaudy nasturtium flowers have a light peppery taste. Why not try pickling their seeds to taste like capers. Even the seed heads from stray Welsh poppies can be used. Once the seeds are extracted they are stirred into many a cake or bread dough.

LEEK TERRINE

Serves 8–10

2.3kg/5lbs leeks, young slender ones if available	8tbsp walnut oil
salt and pepper	2tsp Dijon mustard
	3tbsp wine vinegar
	fresh chervil or dill,
For The Vinaigrette	very finely chopped
8tbsp sunflower oil	

1. Trim the roots and tops of the leeks and remove any withered leaves. Slit the green tops in two lengthwise and wash carefully under running water to get rid of any traces of grit or mud. Tie the leeks in small bundles.

2. Drop the leeks into a large quantity of boiling salted water. Cover the pan until the water returns to the boil then simmer, uncovered, for about 8 minutes or until the leeks are tender. Refresh in a large bowl of iced water and drain on clean tea towels.

3. Line a 26 x 10.5cm/10½ x 4½in hinged loaf tin with cling-film (or an ordinary loaf tin can be used instead). Arrange the leeks in layers in the tin, cutting them to fit if necessary, alternating the rows by using either the dark or the light ends and sprinkling them with salt. Cover the final layer with a weighted board (another loaf tin with a 1.8kg/4lb weight is ideal), set on a plate and refrigerate for at least 4 hours, draining off any liquid that rises from time to time. It also helps to put the tin in the freezer for 1 hour as this makes it easier to cut; but on no account should you allow it to freeze.

4. Meanwhile make the vinaigrette by beating the oils, mustard and vinegar together in a small bowl. Season with salt and pepper.

5. Turn out the loaf carefully by pulling up the cling-film. Keep the terrine wrapped in the cling-film and, using a very sharp thin knife, cut into slices. With the help of a spatula, arrange in the centre of individual plates, then remove the cling-film and, with any luck, it should not fall apart. Spoon the vinaigrette around the leeks and sprinkle the herbs lightly over the vinaigrette.

GRATIN OF SUMMER VEGETABLES

A simple vegetarian dish, its flavour is lifted by the addition of fresh basil.
Serves 6.

6tbsp extra virgin olive oil
plus extra for brushing
2 large red or yellow onions,
thinly sliced
1kg/2.2lbs potatoes,
peeled and thinly sliced
6 medium courgettes,
cut lengthwise into thin slices

450g/1lb fresh tomatoes, sliced
115g/4oz freshly grated
Parmesan or sharp
Cheddar cheese
salt and freshly ground
black pepper
a few leaves of fresh basil

1. Preheat the oven to 180°C/350°F/gas mark 4.

2. Brush a large baking dish with oil. Arrange a layer of onions in the dish, followed by a layer each of potatoes, courgettes and tomatoes. Pour over a little of the oil and sprinkle with a little of the cheese. Season with salt and pepper.

3. Repeat until all the vegetables are used up. Using your hands tear the basil leaves into pieces and poke them into the vegetables. Pour over about 3tbsp of water and finish with a final layer of cheese. Drizzle over the remaining olive oil.

4. Bake for about 1 hour in the preheated oven or until the vegetables are tender when pierced with a knife. If the top begins to brown too much, cover with a sheet of foil while cooking.

MAIN COURSES

Pasta With
Roast Tomato Sauce

For a successful fresh tomato sauce, you have to use the right-flavoured tomatoes.
Most cook/gardeners have their favourites – and to be fair it is a question of
colour, shape, and size as well as whether you grow under glass or indoors – but
I believe for sheer depth of fleshy fruitiness, nothing beats a 'Marmande'. Serves 4.

800g/1 ¾ lb ripe tomatoes
3tbsp extra virgin olive oil,
   plus extra for brushing
large pinch of sugar
salt and black pepper
450g/1lb short pasta,
   such as fusilli or penne

1 clove of garlic,
   peeled and lightly crushed
6-8 fresh basil leaves,
   torn into pieces
85g/3oz shaved slivers
   of fresh Parmesan cheese

1. Preheat the oven to 190°C/375°F/gas mark 5.

2. Using the point of a sharp knife, make a couple of nicks in the skins of the tomatoes. Put them in a bowl and pour over boiling water and leave for a couple of minutes. Drain and peel off the skins. Cut the tomatoes in half and arrange on a lightly oiled baking tray, cut side up. Brush with olive oil, sprinkle with sugar and season with salt and pepper. Roast in the oven for about 50 minutes or until the edges of the tomatoes are slightly blackened.

3. Scrape the tomatoes and all the juices into a food processor and whizz for a couple of seconds to make a sauce with some texture left in it. Pour into a saucepan and taste for seasoning.

4. Cook the pasta in a large saucepan of lightly salted water until just tender.

5. To finish the sauce, heat the 3 tablespoons of olive oil with the crushed garlic in a separate pan until the garlic turns golden. Remove from the heat, discard the garlic, which should still be just in one piece, and stir the oil into the tomato sauce. Keep hot.

6. Once the pasta is cooked, drain and turn it out into a heated serving dish. Pour over the sauce and toss it thoroughly. Sprinkle over the basil and serve with slivers of Parmesan scattered on top.

PASTA WITH
SPRING VEGETABLE SAUCE

Baby turnips, sprigs of young cauliflowers or broccoli, pencil-thin sweetcorn, new potatoes – virtually any and everything can mix together to make a glorious sauce. Use baby broad beans and just toss them whole into the sauce.

450g/1lb pasta,
* such as tagliatelle*
55g/2oz shelled broad beans
6tbsp extra-virgin olive oil
3 spring onions, trimmed
* and cut into 2.5cm/1in slices*
2 baby leeks, trimmed
* and cut into 2.5cm/1in slices*
4tbsp coarsely chopped
* flat-leaf parsley*

3 green peppercorns
2tbsp chicken stock or water
3tbsp white wine
6 baby carrots
55g/2oz mange-tout peas
55g/2oz shelled baby peas
30g/1oz baby spinach leaves
1tbsp balsamic vinegar
sea salt and freshly ground pepper

1. Cook the pasta in a large saucepan of lightly salted water until just tender.

2. While the pasta is cooking, put the broad beans in a saucepan, cover with lightly salted water and bring to the boil over a medium heat. Simmer for 3-4 minutes. Drain and refresh immediately under cold running water. When they are cool enough to handle, skin the beans with your hands by gently slitting them open with the nails and carefully pressing them out with the fingers.

3. Heat 3 tablespoons of the oil in a large pan over a medium to low heat. Add the spring onions, leeks, ½ tablespoon of the parsley and the peppercorns and cook gently for 2-3 minutes. Pour in the stock and white wine and simmer for 1 minute. Stir in the carrots, mange-tout and peas and poach for a further 2-3 minutes. Add the prepared broad beans, drop the baby spinach leaves into the pan and leave them just long enough to wilt.

3. Using a slotted spoon, transfer the vegetables to a warm bowl. Turn up the heat to medium, add the remaining oil and balsamic vinegar and simmer for about 3-4 minutes to allow the sauce to reduce slightly. Season to taste.

4. Serve the pasta in a heated serving dish. Add the vegetables, pour over the sauce, sprinkle with the remaining parsley, and toss.

GRILLED CHICKEN JOINTS
WITH LETTUCE SAUCE

It is a pity that more people do not cook with lettuce; apart from being a sensible way of dealing with the bolted plants, lettuce has such a delightful, clear sweetness. I love to use it in sauces, or wrapped around fish or poultry to keep it moist, or even braised on its own as a vegetable. Serves 4.

8 chicken drumsticks
or thigh portions

Marinade
5 tbsp olive oil
juice of 1 lemon
1 tbsp chervil, chopped
salt and freshly ground
black pepper

Sauce
55g/2oz unsalted butter
1 small bunch of spring onions,
chopped
1 small Cos lettuce, chopped
30ml/3tbsp white wine
2 tbsp crème fraîche
1 tbsp chervil, chopped

1. Using a sharp knife, slash the skin of the chicken joints and put them in a suitable bowl for marinading. Mix the olive oil together with the lemon juice, chervil, salt and pepper and pour over the chicken. Leave to stand for a couple of hours.

2. To cook the chicken, preheat the grill and remove the chicken pieces from the marinade. Grill for about 12-15 minutes, basting occasionally with the marinade and turning them so they cook evenly.

3. Meanwhile to make the sauce, melt the butter over a low heat, add the spring onions and sweat for a couple of minutes until soft. Add the lettuce and stir until coated in the butter. Pour in the white wine, cover the pan and simmer for a further 5-7 minutes, or until the lettuce has softened.

4. Whizz the sauce in the food processor until smooth. With the machine still running, add the chervil and pour in the crème fraîche. Season and serve with the chicken.

TURKEY ESCALOPES WITH REDCURRANTS AND THYME

When cooking redcurrants, never use too high a heat or cook them for too long or they will burst their skins. Serves 4.

4 turkey escalopes weighing about 115g/4oz each
2tbsp flour
salt and freshly ground black pepper
50g/2oz butter

170g/6oz fresh redcurrants, picked from the stems
2 spring onions, finely chopped
grated zest of ½ orange
sprig of fresh thyme
100ml/3 ½fl oz white wine

1. Using a rolling pin, pound the turkey escalopes lightly to flatten. Season the flour and dredge the escalopes so they are lightly covered.

2. Heat the butter in a large frying pan. Add the escalopes, and sauté until just done, about 3-4 minutes on each side. Using a slotted spoon, remove them on to a heated serving platter and keep warm.

3. Using a wooden spoon scrape up any juices from the bottom of the pan, then add the redcurrants with the spring onions, orange zest and thyme. Pour in the white wine, turn up the heat and cook for about 2-3 minutes or until the wine is reduced by about half. Spoon the sauce over the escalopes and serve.

GRILLED DUCK BREASTS WITH HONEY-GLAZED TURNIPS

For this recipe you may prefer teeny-weeny baby turnips with their less pronounced turnip taste. If so, leave them whole without even attempting to peel them. It goes without saying that the larger the turnip – and indeed any vegetable – the more preparation it needs and the longer it takes to cook. Serves 4.

350g/12oz medium turnips,
  peeled
45g/1½oz butter
2tbsp sunflower oil
3tbsp honey
salt and freshly ground
  black pepper

2tsp cider vinegar (optional)
4 duck breasts, weighing about
115g/4oz each
3tbsp chopped parsley

1. Pre heat the grill.

2. Cut the turnips in half and then into slices about 1cm/½in thick.

3. Heat the butter with the oil and honey until melted. Turn up the heat and stir until the mixture turns a rich caramel colour. Add the turnips and stir until they are coated with the syrup. Season with salt and pepper. Cover the pan, lower the heat and simmer until the turnips are cooked through, about 5-8 minutes. If you like a sweet-sour flavour add the vinegar.

4. Meanwhile trim the duck breasts and remove the skin and fat. Season and grill for about 3 minutes on each side, so they are still quite pink.

5. Stir the parsley into the turnips and serve with the duck breasts.

POACHED FILLET OF BEEF

A favourite recipe that relies on two simple, straightforward principles. Use the best possible quality ingredients and cook them as plainly as possible to enhance their inherent flavour. It works. Serves 2.

1tbsp olive oil
285g/10oz fillet steak
salt and freshly ground
*   black pepper*
400ml/14fl oz beef
*   or vegetable stock*
6-8 small new potatoes
1 carrot, sliced

1 celery stalk, sliced
1 leek, sliced
2 pickling onions
sprig of rosemary
2-3 black peppercorns
115g/4oz baby spinach leaves
1tsp fresh horseradish, grated
5tbsp double cream

1. Heat the olive oil in sauté pan, add the steak and season with salt and pepper. Cook over a high heat for a couple of minutes to seal it and remove.

2. Pour in the stock, add the potatoes and simmer for about 5 minutes. Then add the fillet with the carrot, celery, leek, onions, rosemary, peppercorns and a small pinch of salt. Turn down the heat, cover the pan and simmer for about 5 minutes.

3. Stir in the spinach, cover and simmer for about another 3 minutes or until the meat is tender. Using a slotted spoon, transfer the meat and vegetables to a serving dish and keep warm.

4. To make a sauce, strain about 200ml/7fl oz of the stock into a separate pan. Turn up the heat and cook to reduce the liquid by half. Turn down the heat, stir in the horseradish and cream and simmer for 2-3 minutes. Adjust the seasoning.

5. To serve, cut the beef into thin slices and arrange on a plate surrounded by the vegetables with the sauce poured over the top.

Braised Pork With Fennel, Apple And Juniper Berries

*I prefer to cook with certain dessert rather than cooking apples
as their flavour is generally more complex. Provided you choose a variety
that holds together well – like a 'Cox's Orange Pippin' or an 'Egremont Russet'–
it works. Depending on how well trimmed the joint of pork is, you may well need
to skim the fat before adding the cream to make the sauce. Serves 6.*

450ml/¾pt dry apple cider	3 fennel bulbs, quartered
1.35kg/3lb boned leg	3 apples, peeled,
or loin of free-range pork	cored and thickly sliced
salt and freshly ground	8-10 juniper berries,
black pepper	lightly crushed
2tbsp oil	3tbsp apple brandy (Calvados)
15g/½oz butter	1tbsp flour
3 medium onions, sliced	100ml/3½fl oz double cream

1. Preheat the oven to 180°C/350°F/gas mark 4.

2. Put the cider in a pan, turn up the heat and boil to reduce the liquid by half. Set aside.

3. Rub the meat all over with salt and pepper, trimming off any excess fat. Heat the oil with the butter and brown the meat on all sides. Remove from the pan, add the onions and stir until the onions soften slightly.

4. Add the fennel, apple and juniper berries. Season and stir until the fennel begins to take on colour. Scrape the mixture into a heavy flame-proof casserole and set the pork on top. In a separate pan, heat the apple brandy, set it alight and pour over the meat while still flaming. Sift in the flour and pour over the reduced cider.

5. Bring the casserole to a simmer on top of the stove before covering and placing in the oven. Cook for about 1½ hours or until the meat is tender.

6. Lift out the meat and carve into thin slices. Add the cream to the casserole and, stirring continuously, heat gently on top of the stove. Adjust the seasoning and serve the meat surrounded by the vegetables in the sauce.

SWORDFISH KEBAB

Although I usually insist on fresh herbs, this is one occasion when you can use
dried bay leaves. Just remember to soak them for at least one hour
in boiling water to soften them. Serves 6.

675g/1½lb swordfish
or fresh tunny

Marinade
1tsp chilli paste
1tsp tomato paste
3tbsp olive oil plus extra
for the bay leaves

juice and grated rind of 1 lemon
2 shallots, finely chopped
2 cloves garlic, crushed
30 bay leaves
salt and freshly ground
black pepper to taste

1. Prepare the fish by, if necessary, skinning and filleting it.
   Then cut into 2.5cm/1in cubes and put into a suitable bowl for marinating.

2. To make the marinade, mix the chilli and tomato pastes together.
   Then slowly beat in the olive oil, add the lemon juice and rind, and stir in the
   shallots and garlic. Season and pour over the prepared fish. Leave to marinate
   for at least a couple of hours in a cool place.

3. If you are using fresh bay leaves, using a pastry brush simply paint them all over
   lightly with olive oil. If you are using dried bay leaves, leave them to soak in
   boiling water for about 1 hour to soften, then pat them dry and coat with olive
   oil as above.

4. Preheat the grill. Drain the fish, reserving the marinade. To assemble the kebab
   sticks, start each one with a bay leaf, then add a cube of fish, and carry on alternating each cube with a bayleaf until you finish with a final bay leaf. Brush over
   the marinade lightly. Cook under the preheated grill for about 10 minutes,
   turning occasionally and painting the fish with the marinade to prevent it from
   drying out.

MONKFISH WITH HERB-DRESSED SORREL

One of Alistair Little's recipes from his award winning Keep It Simple,
I was lucky enough to have him cook it specially for me when recording
for Woman's Hour. Working with Alistair in his kitchen was not only fun but
an inspiration. Serves 4.

300ml/½pt dry white wine
1 shallot, coarsely chopped
salt and freshly ground
*   black pepper*
150ml/¼pt double cream
bunch of dill
bunch of flat leaf parsley,
*   stems removed, coarsely chopped*
4-5 tarragon leaves,
coarsely chopped

bunch of chives, coarsely chopped
450g/1lb sorrel, stalks removed
1 monkfish tail, weighing about
*   450g/1lb*
55g/2oz flour
2tbsp sunflower oil
225g/8oz unsalted butter,
*   chilled and cut into small cubes*

1. To make the sauce put the wine with the shallot in a large saucepan. Season with salt and pepper. Cook over a high heat until the wine has almost completely evaporated.

2. Stir in the cream off the heat and cook to reduce to a syrupy consistency.

3. Meanwhile whizz the dill with the parsley, tarragon and chives until finely chopped in a food processor. Add the sauce and carry on whizzing until you have a smooth green purée. Set aside to cool.

4. Pick over the sorrel leaves. Place 5 or 6 leaves on top of each other, roll them up into a cigar shape and cut across them to make fine strips.

5. Cut the monkfish fillet into 4 escalopes through the skin and at an angle of 30 degrees, starting towards the tail end. Season the flour and dredge the escalopes so they are lightly covered and coated evenly. Shake off any excess flour.

6. Heat the sunflower oil in a suitable pan and sauté the escalopes, skin side down, for about 2 minutes. Turn them carefully and give them 1 minute on the other

side or until cooked. Transfer the cooked escalopes to a warmed plate.

7. Return the sauce to a clean pan and simmer, taking care not to boil or overcook it or you will lose its glorious green colour. Swirl in the small pieces of butter, off the heat, 4 or 5 at a time, gently rotating the pan to melt them in. Or, if you prefer, you can beat in the butter, a few pieces at a time using a small hand whisk or a wooden spoon. Keep warm on the lowest possible heat.

8. Transfer the sauce to a large bowl, drop in the prepared sorrel and toss swiftly. If you have the temperature right the sauce will coat the sorrel leaves completely, leaving no free sauce in the pan.

9. To serve, place a mound of sorrel in the centre of 4 warm plates. Place a piece of the fish on top of each mound and serve at once.

VEGETABLES
AND SALADS

MIXED LEAF SALAD

Creating a salad – picking, choosing and mixing the leaves, herbs or vegetables – is one of the great pleasures of preparing a meal. But then I adore salads.

What goes into a salad depends on the time of the year, what is in season – either from the garden or the shops – the taste and colours you like. In winter, I tend to go for harsher salads with bitter sharp flavours. Plenty of endive, Belgian chicory, frisée, water or land cress and the range of gloriously vibrant red to purple Italian chicory. During the summer, my salads are lighter, prettier and sweeter. Perhaps there will be copious quantities of nutty chervil just picked from the herb patch or juicy purslaine. Often there is plenty of rocket with a hint of peppery fieriness cut by the lemon sharpness of baby sorrel leaves; for a gentler sweeter succulence there are 'Little Gem' lettuces and the soft silky 'Cut and Come Again' leaves. The crispness of a 'Webb's Wonderful' is always a delight particularly when contrasted with a juicy Cos; in fact the range of flavours, textures and colours of lettuces never ceases to amaze. There are no recipes, no correct proportions, only what you like and what you enjoy to eat.

In season, I will probably throw in a few flowers – nasturtium are strikingly bold both in colour and taste whereas hyssop is far more retiring but equally inter-esting. I might add a few poppy seeds from the wild poppies that inevitably grow in the vegetable patch, or radish pods picked just as they begin to form for a tender texture and the mildest of mild radish flavours.

For a Vinaigrette always choose as good an olive oil as you can possibly afford. An extra virgin will make the difference in depth and richness of flavour. A good quality vinegar is equally important, try a white wine or cider vinegar or one that you have already infused with herbs or flowers (see page 77). The basic propor-tions are 5 parts olive oil to 1 part vinegar, but first take a teaspoon of Dijon mustard and beat it in a bowl. Slowly add a few drops of olive oil – starting it off as you would a mayonnaise by beating it into the mustard – then whisk in the rest of the oil with the vinegar and season with freshly ground black pepper and sea salt. To vary the flavour you can add a few chopped fresh herbs – flat leaf parsley, tarragon, chives – or a clove of chopped garlic.

To add extra texture or colour to a salad, try tossing in crushed walnuts or lightly sauté in flaked almonds or pine kernels in olive oil, then scatter them over the salad. Crumble in a piece of young goat's cheese or even a small chunk of Stilton; use up any stale bread by frying it in olive oil to make croutons then add these to the salad. No meal should ever be without one.

ROAST GARLIC

It's extraordinary that roast garlic hardly tastes like garlic at all – it is far
creamier and milder without any of its usual pungency. Serves 6.

6 heads of garlic   *olive oil, for brushing*

1. Preheat the oven to 180°C/350°F/gas mark 4.
2. Using a pastry brush, paint each head of garlic all over with olive oil. Cut out 6 small squares of greaseproof paper and wrap up each garlic head in one. Bake them in the preheated oven for about 35 minutes, or until soft.
3. To extract the purée, simply slit the skin of a clove with a knife and ease out the pulp or press down on it to squeeze it out. Serve with roasted meats.

FLAT LEAF PARSLEY SALAD

The inspiration for making this salad with flat leaf parsley came from
Alistair Little, one of our innovative British chefs. Serves 4.

Rub a salad bowl with a cut garlic clove. Finely chop the 12 stoned black olives with 4 sweet anchovies and 1tbsp drained capers. Put them in the salad bowl with a finely sliced small red onion. Pour in 5tbsp extra virgin olive oil and 1tbsp wine vinegar and a few grindings of black pepper. Mix well and allow to stand for at least 30 minutes. Pick the leaves from the stems of a large bunch of flat leaf, wash and spin them dry. Just before serving, toss the parsley in the bowl with the other ingredients. Serve with shavings of fresh Parmesan.

SALSA FRESCA

Salsa is the Mexicans' answer to pesto. For a typical fieriness, salsas almost always contain chillies in some form or another and are usually served chilled with grilled meats or fish or the inevitable corn chips.
As with pesto, the combination and proportions of ingredients vary. Fresh coriander leaves are popular, but I have swopped them for a far more British herb – mint.

4 spring onions, chopped
8 plum tomatoes, chopped
2 fresh green chillies, finely sliced
small bunch fresh mint, chopped

1 tsp sugar (optional)
juice of ½ lime
sea salt

1. Mix the spring onions in a bowl with the tomatoes, chillies and mint. Stir in the sugar, lime juice and about 3 tablespoons water – or just enough to moisten the salsa. Season to taste. If the tomatoes are sharp, you can add a little extra sugar but make sure the salsa is not overly sweet.

2. Chill in the refrigerator for at least 30 minutes before serving.

HERB PESTO

In Italy the 'real thing' is made with basil, pine nuts and olive oil. Some people add garlic, others insist on Parmesan but there is no disputing the first three ingredients. Here in Britain where, because of the climate, basil does not grow so easily or in such profusion, it makes sense to use a different herb or a combination of herbs. While we are ringing the changes, why not vary the nuts and substitute walnuts or almonds for the pine nuts?

To make enough pesto for four people, first either pound by hand or whizz in the food processor 50g/2oz of walnuts or almonds or hazelnuts. Then add the herbs. These could be flat leaf or curly parsley, marjoram or coriander and you will need a surprisingly huge amount, a generous bunch at the very least. Once the herbs are finely chopped, you can stir in the olive oil. For that quantity of nuts and herbs about 150ml/¼ pint is a guide line; but you may need more if you want a thinner pesto. Finally season with salt and lashings of black pepper and pour over the pasta. It is ready.

You may want to add a couple of garlic cloves and an ounce or two of freshly grated Parmesan, although frankly I think they crowd the flavour of the herbs. Far better to keep our own-made pesto fresh and punched with herbs.

For an insider's view on chillis – or chiles as he would have us call them – you can do no better than consult Mark Miller's *The Great Chile Book* (Ten Speed Press). He claims there are 'as many as 150–200 different varieties of chiles that have been positively identified... in addition there are undoubtedly some rare varieties growing in remote regions of Mexico or South America that have yet to be discovered'.

He goes on to clarify the different spellings. Chile means the plant or pod; chilli – the traditional dish containing meat and chiles (and sometimes beans); and chilli – the commercial spice powder. But even then you shouldn't 'count on it'. Mark Miller, chef at The Coyote Café in Santa Fe, uses in his kitchen 'some 20 different types including Anaheims, Fresnos, New Mexico greens and reds, polanos, serranos, jalapenos and habaneros'. As for which ones to use 'in general, the smaller the chile, the hotter it is; this is because smaller chiles have a larger amount of seeds and vein (or internal rib) relative to larger chiles'. These, evidently, are the parts that contain the heat so if you are likely to be troubled by the fieriness, scoop out the seeds and de-vein the chile before you start cooking.

VEGETABLE CRISPS

Crisps – or rather vegetable crisps – are all the rage. And they are such a simple idea that it makes you wonder why we have not been making them for years. Basically they are exactly the same as potato crisps, only made with vegetables.

Not just any old vegetables, you understand, but ones that fry quickly and easily without absorbing too much fat while still keeping their texture. Into this category surprisingly enough falls beetroot, artichokes stripped down to their hearts, parsnips, sweet potatoes and celeriac.

To prepare them, all you do is to peel and wash whichever vegetables you choose; but, and this is a very important but, never be tempted to leave them soaking in water as this will dissipate the starch. Then slice them finely. Think how thin a potato crisp is and then you will realise just how they ought to be. A slicing disc on a food processor makes life a lot easier, failing that a very sharp knife or a swing vegetable peeler. I have also tried cutting them like proper chips – into long thin strips – and they work equally well but just need a longer cooking time.

Once you have prepared the vegetables, you need to heat the oil – preferably a vegetable or corn oil – to 190°C/375°F. The way to test the temperature is to drop in a small cube of bread; if it browns in about 40 seconds, you know the oil is hot enough. Fry your vegetables in batches; never overcrowd the pan as it lowers the temperature of the oil and makes frying much more difficult. Drain the crisps on paper towels and season liberally with sea salt – and they are ready. Finally remember to wait until the oil has heated up to the correct temperature before you start frying the next batch. Once you have got the hang of it – what could be simpler?

ROAST VEGETABLES

Most firm vegetables can be roasted. In winter you can ring the changes by using parsnips, swedes, potatoes, salsify, turnips or Jerusalem artichokes. Remember to cut the slices the same thickness so that all the vegetables roast at more or less the same speed. Serves 4–6.

1 fennel bulb, trimmed and sliced
1 red pepper, de-seeded and sliced
1 yellow pepper,
  de-seeded and sliced
2 medium onions,
  peeled and sliced
2 medium tomatoes, sliced
3 leeks, sliced
3 ears of fresh corn, sliced

8 cloves of garlic, peeled and sliced
225g/8oz potatoes,
  scrubbed and sliced
100ml/3 ½fl oz extra
  virgin olive oil
3-4 sprigs of thyme
3-4 sprigs of rosemary
sea salt and freshly
  ground black pepper

1. Preheat the oven to 190°C/375°F/gas mark 5.

2. Spread the vegetables, mixing them up together, in a shallow roasting tray large enough to accommodate them in a single layer.

3. Pour over the olive oil, turning the vegetables to thoroughly coat them on all sides. Tuck in the sprigs of herbs, sprinkle over the sea salt and finish with several grindings of pepper.

4. Roast, turning the vegetables occasionally, for about 1½ hours or until tender when pierced with the point of a knife.

MASH ITALIAN-STYLE

For every potato dish, the right variety is important; so for the lightest, smoothest mash choose a floury potato such as 'Pentland Dell' or a mature 'Maris Bard'. Never overwork the potatoes by puréeing them in a food processor – you will end up with glue. Instead use an old-fashioned masher and then beat in the liquids for the final touch. Serves 4.

675g/1½lbs potatoes,
  peeled and diced
4 cloves of garlic, peeled
6tbsp olive oil

75ml/5tbsp single cream
salt and freshly ground
  black pepper

1. Put the potatoes in a saucepan with the garlic and water to cover. Add 2 table-spoons of the olive oil and boil until tender. Drain, reserving about a 150ml/¼pt of the cooking water.

2. Mash the potatoes with the garlic cloves. For a milder flavour discard at least two, if not more. Beat in the remaining oil and the cream and, if you prefer a looser textured, softer mash, add a little of the reserved cooking water. Season to taste.

Variations:

1. Substitute 30g/1oz freshly grated Parmesan for the cream; but make sure you add enough of the cooking water to moisten the mash.

2. Instead of using just potatoes, try half the quantity of potatoes and half parsnips.

3. Another interesting combination is potato mixed with celeriac. In this case use about 450g/1lb potatoes to 225g/8oz celeriac.

4. Alternatively you can make champ. Make the mash as above and then fold in about 115-170g/4-6oz chopped cooked spring greens or cabbage.

Potatoes are made up mostly of carbohydrate and fibre with vitamins A and C, iron and calcium. Once cooked what affects their actual texture is the proportion of starch to dry matter; it follows that a waxy potato with its lower starch content will boil and deep-fry superbly but is useless for baking or mashing; a floury potato, on the other hand, is ideal for mash but will probably fall apart when boiled.

This is why it is so important to choose the right potato for the right job, whether you are boiling, steaming, baking, roasting, mashing or chipping. Our potatoes fall into three categories – earlies from the beginning of June, second earlies from July to September and maincrop that are ready for harvesting from August onwards.

Earlies or new potatoes, when they are first lifted, have a very high dry matter/low starch content so they are perfect for boiling; but remember as they mature the starch content rises and their waxiness disappears. One way of checking their age is to rub the skin with your finger; it should flake off as they should be too young for any 'skin set'.

Recently much fuss – and rightly so – has been made of some of the continental salad varieties with their remarkable nutty flavours and firm textures; amongst my favourites are 'Belle de Fontenay', 'Linzer Dalikatess' and 'Ratte'.

POTATO CAKES

For the best of all potato pancakes, choose a starchy potato that holds together well
– Maris Piper or King Edward. To make sure you allow the cakes plenty of room
to spread, use a suitably wide based sauté or frying pan; mine is a 20cm/8inch
non-stick pan. Serves 4.

450g/1lb potatoes (see above)
1 small onion
salt and freshly ground
   black pepper

small bunch of flat leaf parsley,
   chopped
2tbsp butter
4tbsp olive oil

1. Peel the potatoes but do not soak them in water or the starch will be removed. Coarsely grate the potatoes with the onion, mix with the parsley and season.

2. Heat half of the oil and butter in a suitable pan. Spread a layer of potatoes on the bottom of the pan. Press it down quite firmly to form a cake about 1cm/½inch thick and cook over medium heat until the underside is golden brown, shaking the pan occasionally to prevent the cake from sticking. Remember, as the potatoes cook it will form a solid mass.

3. When the underside is cooked, either flip the cake over onto the other side using a spatula, or turn it onto a plate and slide it back into the pan with the uncooked side facing down. Reduce the heat slightly and cook until the underside is brown. If the potatoes do not seem to be cooking through, it helps to cover the pan for a few minutes.

4. When the cake is cooked, remove it from the pan and keep warm. Add more fat to the pan and continue with another cake.

ASPARAGUS WITH PARMESAN

Nothing could be more straightforward than roasting asparagus as all you need is a roasting pan and an oven. Use whatever size asparagus you have to hand – you will have to adjust the cooking time according to how thick or thin the spears are – and make sure they are fresh, taut and tightly budded. Serves 4.

450g/1lb asparagus
4-6tbsp olive oil
sea salt

juice of ½ lemon
freshly grated Parmesan to serve
(optional)

1. Preheat the oven to 180°C/350°F/gas mark 4.

2. Trim the asparagus quite tightly, cutting off any woody ends of stems. In fact just to be on the safe side – and to save yourself the trouble of peeling the stems – trim them right up to where they turn green.

3. Using a pastry brush, paint the base of a large ovenproof dish or roasting tin with olive oil and sprinkle with sea salt. Arrange the asparagus on top, coat them generously with the olive oil and sprinkle with a little more salt. Use your hands to toss and turn them to make sure they are covered all over with the oil.

4. Roast in the pre-heated oven for between 10-18 minutes, depending on how thick the asparagus are, until tender. Keep a close watch during the last few minutes as they are critical. If the asparagus are left too long, the tips can catch and almost 'fry' and turn crispy – not a particularly desirable state of affairs.

5. To serve, toss in the lemon juice and, if required, scatter with thin shavings of Parmesan.

RATATOUILLE

Eat it hot or cold, with baked fish, grilled or roast meat, on its own or mixed with a couple of beaten eggs and baked in the oven – there is no end to the joys of well cooked ratatouille. Serves 6.

Heat 4tbsp olive oil in a pan and sauté a large, thinly sliced onion for about 5-7 minutes or until translucent.

Add 6 ripe tomatoes, cut into quarters with a pinch of sugar if required, and two medium aubergines, sliced and quartered. Cover the pan and cook for 5 minutes or until the tomatoes begin to give up their juice.

GREEN BEANS WITH TOMATOES

One of the delights of summer is picking young beans from the vegetable patch, you can be sure they are fresh, tender and need no stringing. Here is my method of dealing with the beans as they grow older.

450g/1lb fresh French beans
3tbsp olive oil
1 medium onion, finely sliced
325g/12oz fresh or canned

plum tomatoes, peeled
and finely chopped
5 or 6 leaves of fresh basil
salt and black pepper

1. Snap or cut the stem end off the beans. Wash in cold water and drain.

2. Heat the oil in a large frying pan. Add the onion and cook for 5-6 minutes until soft. Add the tomatoes and simmer for a further 6-8 minutes until softened.

3. Pour in 125ml/4fl oz water. Season and add the basil. Stir in the beans, turning them in the pan so they are thoroughly coated with the sauce. Cover the pan and simmer for about 15-20 minutes or until tender, stirring occasionally. If the sauce starts to dry out, you can always add a little extra water. Serve hot or cold.

I'm always astonished when I hear of gardeners growing aubergines in this country – I thought we didn't have the climate; but provided they are well protected there is, apparently, no problem.

What does seem more problematic is whether to salt the aubergines or not. I remember endless recipes where detailed instructions were given on how to slice them, sprinkle them with salt, and leave them for an hour, preferably weighted, to exude their juice.

Frankly I've never seen the point. In spite of what several chefs or cookery writers say, aubergines are not bitter; you do not need to get rid of their water – it's a waste of time, delays cooking and tends to discolour them before you have even started. The only very marginal advantage is that once they have been salted, they tend to soak up less oil; however most cooks I know would actually consider this a disadvantage as if you are using a good olive oil, you want its flavour to come through.

PUDDINGS

SUMMER PUDDING

*As a closet traditionalist, I insist on a Summer Pudding made
in the straightforward, old-fashioned way. Day-old white bread (although
I know plenty of cooks who insist on granary or wholemeal), buckets of the
summer's soft fruit, sugar to sweeten, a dash of Blackcurrant cordial and white
wine to heighten the flavours – and that's it.*

*Which fruit you use is the tricky part. Some people adore strawberries;
I find their flavour far too intrusive and their texture, after twenty
four hours, rather slimey – they just don't hold well together, and as for their
pips, in a Summer Pudding they drive me mad. So you might find it rather
inconsistent if I say raspberries are perfectly acceptable because they hold their
texture, as do blackberries, once the summer has deepened and they ripen on the
bushes. Plums do not work
neither do cherries, their texture is just not right. Gooseberries are another
addition with which I don't hold much store, they are the wrong colour and a
Summer Pudding should be made with red fruit, or at least in various shades
from pale pink to deep purple. Don't ask me why, it has always been that
way and, as far as I'm concerned, it should stay that way.*

*So which fruit can you use? Any of the currants (white currants are
my exception to prove the rule), any berries – raspberries, blueberries,
blackberries, loganberries, and any of those amazing hybrids and crosses
such as jostaberries, marionberries, sunberries, tayberries,
tummelberries or woosterberries.*

Of course you must make up your own mind – and I hope you will.

Serves 8–10

Day-old white bread, crusts
removed and cut into
5mm/¼in thick slices
900g/2lb black or red
or white currants, raspberries

or blackberries (see opposite)
115g/4oz caster sugar
1tbsp blackcurrant cordial
2tbsp white wine

1. Cut a circle from one slice of bread to fit the bottom of a 1.5l/2½pint pudding basin. Then cut the rest into wedges to fit around the side. Every gap must be filled with bread otherwise the pudding will not hold together.

2. Meanwhile put the fruit with the sugar, blackcurrant cordial and white wine in a saucepan. Simmer gently for about 5 minutes or until the fruit softens slightly. Leave to cool.

3. Using a slotted spoon, ladle the fruit into the bowl, packing it quite tightly so it comes right up to the top. Cover with a couple of layers of bread, trimming the edges for a tidy finish. Pour over the juice, then weight the pudding by putting a plate on top with a couple of kitchen weights or heavy tins. Put it in the refrigerator and leave overnight, or longer if you prefer.

4. To turn the pudding out, run a thin knife between the pudding and the basin, put a serving dish upside down on top and turn it over quickly, giving it a quick, sharp shake.

OPEN FRUIT TARTS

<u>SERVES 6-8</u>

Instead of going to the trouble of making your own pastry, try buying a packet of Filo pastry instead. It is one of the best kept secrets as it is so simple and quick to use. Then you fill the tart with fruit – either freshly picked or lightly poached in a sugar syrup – and bake it in the oven. It really is as easy that.

Take a 25.5cm/10in spring-form cake tin and brush the inside lavishly all over with melted butter. Spread out one sheet of filo pastry to cover the base, allowing the edge to tumble over the edge of the tin. Brush this all over with melted butter, then lay another sheet on top, making sure that the excess filo does not overlap too much as you want to be able to fold it over to make a rim. Carry on adding another layer and brushing with butter until you have totalled about six layers. You must work quickly as filo tends to dry out and become quite brittle rather fast – one tip is to lay a damp tea towel on top of the pastry which will keep it fresh for longer while you are working with it.

Once you have finished with the filo, add the fruit. A couple of suggestions are 67g/1½lb halved and stoned plums sprinkled with pelargonium sugar (see page 76) or 675g/1½lb stoned and sliced apricots poached in a sugar syrup made with 115g/4oz sugar, a teaspoon of ground cinnamon and 150ml/¼pt water. Once the fruit is ready, you arrange it on the filo, dot it with a generous 30g/1oz butter, roll up the excess filo to form a rim around the fruit and bake the tart in a pre heated oven 190°C/375°F/gas mark 5.

You can also bake the filo blind – that is to say without any fruit filling. Just make sure the base is thoroughly weighted down with baking beans; once it is cooked it can be filled with fresh strawberries, raspberries, red, white or black currants, sprinkled with icing sugar and served with lashings of cream.

FRUIT KEBABS
WITH FLAVOURED BUTTERS

I first discovered Fruit Kebabs when writing *10-Minute Cuisine* with Marie-Pierre Moine. For an easy-to-prepare, quick but effective, pudding they are just the ticket. You can use any firm-textured fruit – home-grown, tropical or Mediterranean. The secret is to choose fruit that does not collapse while cooking. Try whole strawberries, grapes and kumquats, halved apricots, figs and plums, slices of pear, apple and guava, thick slices from a firm (not quite ripe) banana, segments of orange, grapefruit, clementine and mandarin and chunks of pineapple.

Prepare the fruit by washing or wiping it with a damp cloth and cutting it according to your requirements. If it is likely to discolour once it is cut, brush it lightly with lemon juice. The best skewers to use are the thin bamboo ones – metal ones might taint or discolour the fruit. To assemble, all you do is to thread the prepared fruit on to the skewers. Do not pack them too tightly on the sticks and arrange them with an eye for the tastes, colours and shapes of the fruit.

To make sure they stay juicy and succulent, just before grilling brush the kebabs with a sweet butter (see below). Then pop them under a preheated grill and grill for no more than a couple of minutes on each side, just enough to melt the butter and heat the fruit through.

There are any number of flavoured sweet butters but the most effective, I find, have a dash of alcohol. They are always made on the same principle; softened unsalted butter that is to say, butter that has been out of the refrigerator for at least 30 minutes is mixed with sugar and alcohol. You can make it with a fork or a whisk but, far easier, is to use a food processor.

For a Rum Butter to go with the bananas whizz until smooth 55g/2oz unsalted butter with one tablespoon of rum and one tablespoon of brown sugar. For a Vodka butter to go with strawberries, whizz until smooth 55g/2oz unsalted butter with one tablespoon of vodka, one tablespoon of caster sugar and a few fresh mint leaves. For apples make a Calvados butter with 55g/2oz unsalted butter with one tablespoon of calvados and one tablespoon of brown sugar and for plums a Sherry butter with 55g/2oz unsalted butter with one tablespoon of dry sherry, one tablespoon of brown caster and a pinch of chopped crystallised ginger.

STRAWBERRY MOUSSE IN A CHOCOLATE CASE

*A chocolate case is surprisingly easy to prepare and looks most impressive.
For the most intense of flavours, always try to use strawberry when at their
ripest and juiciest. Serves 8.*

light vegetable oil for greasing	*170g/6oz caster sugar*
170g/6oz plain chocolate	*the juice of 1 lemon*
15g/½oz unsalted butter	*5 x 5ml tsp powdered gelatine*
900g/2lb fresh strawberries	*150 ml/¼pt whipping cream*

1. Oil a 25.5cm/10in x 3.5cm/1½in cake tin with a removable base. Line the base with oiled greaseproof paper.

2. Melt the chocolate with 5 tablespoons of water in the top of a double saucepan set over hot water. When the chocolate has melted, stir in the butter and keep stirring until it too has melted. Spoon the chocolate over the base of the tin and spread evenly with a spatula all over the bottom and up the sides. Wipe the rim carefully and refrigerate.

3. Meanwhile hull the strawberries and wash if necessary. Whizz in a food processor or blender to reduce to a purée, then sieve them into a large non-metal bowl. Stir in about three quarters of the sugar and the lemon juice. Taste to see if the remaining sugar is required.

4. Dissolve the gelatine in a small cup according to the instructions on the packet and leave for a few minutes to 'sponge'. Then place the cup in a pan of hot water and heat gently until the gelatine is dissolved. Stir into the strawberry purée and set the bowl in iced water, stirring occasionally until the gelatine begins to set. Lightly whip the cream, fold into the purée, then pour into the chocolate case. Refrigerate and 2 hours before serving, set in the freezer.

5. To unmould, hold a hot tea towel around the sides of the cake tin. Using a sharp thin knife cut down between the chocolate sides and the tin until the chocolate case is loosened enough to push up. Separate the chocolate case from the base of the tin with a palette knife, carefully peeling off the paper. Place on a large flat serving dish and keep refrigerated until serving.

BLACKCURRANT MUFFINS

For the best possible evenly-cooked muffins with a deep body and a nicely puffed crown, use muffin tins with wells about 4cm/1½in deep. And do remember to grease them thoroughly but sparingly – too often an extra-thick coating can ruin the muffin's texture. Makes 18.

115g/4oz unsalted butter plus extra for greasing
170g/6oz granulated sugar
2 eggs
255g/9oz plain flour

2tsp baking powder
a pinch of salt
250ml/8fl oz smetana or buttermilk
225g/8oz blackcurrants

1. Preheat the oven to 180°C/350°F/gas mark 4.

2. Cream the butter and sugar together until soft. In a separate bowl beat the eggs, then gradually incorporate them into the butter and sugar mixture.

3. Sift the flour, baking powder and salt together into a large bowl. Make a well in the centre and add the butter mixture, smetana and the blackcurrants. Stir lightly with a large spoon, just enough to mix the ingredients together. But do not over-mix as – believe it or not – the batter should be lumpy.

4. Grease the bun or muffin tins (see above). Fill the wells two-thirds full with batter and bake in the preheated oven for 20 minutes, or until the muffins have puffed up and browned. Serve warm with lashings of butter or cream cheese.

CARAMELIZED UPSIDE-DOWN PEAR TART

A caramelized pear tart makes a welcome change from the better known tarte tatin made with apples. Choose any firm good-flavoured pear such as the chunky 'Beurré d'Anjou', or the speckled 'Williams Bon Chrétien'. Serves 8.

Pastry
175g/6 oz plain flour
65g/2½oz caster sugar
½tsp salt
100g/3½oz cold unsalted butter,
  cut into cubes
3 egg yolks, beaten

Filling
6-8 firm pears
175g/6oz sugar
115g/4oz unsalted butter

1. Make the pastry by sifting the flour, sugar and salt into a bowl. Rub in the butter using your fingertips. Make a well in the centre of the mixture and pour in the eggs. Mix quickly with a knife to form crumbs, adding a little water if necessary. Press the dough into a ball, wrap in plastic film and leave to rest in the refrigerator for at least 30 minutes.

2. Meanwhile quarter, peel and core the pears and sprinkle over a couple of table-spoons of the sugar.

3. Preheat the oven to 200°C/400°F/gas mark 6.

4. Melt the butter and the remaining sugar in a 24-26cm/9½-10½in heavy-bottomed ovenproof pan. Arrange the fruit in a single layer over the mixture. Cook over a high heat, uncovered, for about 20 minutes, until the sugar starts to caramelize and turns a deep golden brown. Leave to cool.

5. Roll out a thin circle of pastry slightly larger than the pan you are using. Place the pastry on top of the fruit, tucking the dough around the edges.
Bake for 15 minutes, then lower the heat to 180°C/350°F/gas mark 4 and bake for a further 15 minutes.

6. Leave the tart to cool for about 3-5 minutes, then run a knife around the edge to loosen. Put a serving dish upside down on top of the tart and turn it over quickly, giving it a quick, sharp shake so the tart drops on to the dish. If any pears stick to the bottom of the pan remove them with a spatula and replace on the tart. Serve the tart while still warm.

It is said that there are as many known varieties of pears as there are apples – about 5000 in total – but you try finding them.

At a Royal Horticultural Society Conference held in 1888, a talk was given on growing fruit profitably for the market. Several pears were mentioned that rejoiced under such splendid names as Aston Town, Eyewood, Hessel, Williams Bon Chretien, Beurré Capiamont, Beurré d'Amanlis, M. le Curé, Vicar of Wakefield, Doyenne d'Eté, Mme Treyve, Marie Louise d'Uccile, Louise Bonne of Jersey and Marie Louise. And where are they now? Only Williams Bon Chretien is still commercially grown.

Of course I know about the pressures of the market and how the demands of the retailers have changed – the supermarkets want their fruit to be regularly shaped, of an even size, with a good skin finish and a long-shelf life – and only certain varieties will fit that description.

But it is up to all of us lucky enough to have gardens to plant the older varieties, we must preserve them to ensure they do not vanish from our tables. Important work has been carried out to remind everyone about our heritage of apples – but we must not forget our pears.

ANISE POACHED PEARS

*Although I lay no claims to making the original introduction, I think
the marriage of pears to anise is an inspired one as together they make such a
well-balanced match. Serves 6-8.*

6-8 firm dessert pears
the juice of ½ lemon
6tbsp granulated sugar

4 or 5 star anise pods
2tbsp Pernod

1. Peel, halve and core the pears. Toss in a bowl with the lemon juice.

2. Heat the sugar with 450ml/¾pt water in a large saucepan, stirring until the sugar dissolves. Add the star anise and simmer for about 5 minutes.

3. Add the pears to the poaching syrup, turn up the heat and bring it back to the boil. Reduce the heat and simmer for about 10 minutes or until the pears are just tender, turning them occasionally.

4. Using a slotted spoon, lift the pears out of the syrup. Turn up the heat and boil the syrup to reduce by about half. Stir in the Pernod, simmer for a couple of minutes, then pass through a sieve and pour over the pears.

APPLE, BLACKBERRY
AND SCENTED GERANIUM LEAF PIE

*Use smaller leaves from the plant, otherwise they will be too tough and
for a really heady, scented pie, try not only using the scented geranium (pelargonium) leaves but also the flavoured sugar as well (see page 76).*

For 122 cm/9in pie	*300g/10½oz sugar*
1kg/2.2lbs apples	*a pinch of salt*
3tbsp fresh lemon juice	*500g/1lb shortcrust pastry*
450g/1lb blackberries, rinsed	*45g/1½oz butter*
4 scented geranium leaves, rinsed	*1 egg white, beaten*

1. Preheat the oven to 200°C/400°F/gas mark 6.

2. Peel, core and slice the apples. Toss them in the lemon juice, then stir in the blackberries, geranium leaves, sugar and salt and leave to stand.

3. Meanwhile roll out the pastry and use about half to line a pie dish. Spoon in the fruit mixture, spreading it evenly over the pastry and mounding it slightly in the centre. Dot with the butter.

4. Cover the fruit with the remaining pastry, trim and crimp the edges. Glaze the pastry by brushing with the egg white. Using a sharp knife, slash vents in the centre of the pastry lid.

5. Bake in a preheated oven for 45-55 minutes or until the apples are tender when pierced with a knife. If the pastry browns too much cover with butter paper or foil. Serve with whipped or clotted cream.

ELDERBERRY SORBET

Elderflower sorbet – made with the flowerheads infused in a sugar-syrup – is an old favourite I first discovered several years ago in the classic Constance Spry Cookery Book. This version, made with the berries instead, results in a fruitier, brilliant rich-red coloured sorbet.

450g/1lb fresh elderberries
115g/4oz caster sugar
juice of 1 lemon

1. Rinse and pick the elderberries from the stems and whizz in a food processor or liquidizer to make a purée. Pass through a nylon sieve to remove the pips.

2. Heat the sugar with 150ml/¼pt water, stirring until dissolved. Turn up the heat and boil for 4-5 minutes. Then remove from the heat and leave to cool.

3. Pour the cooled syrup into the puréed fruit with half of the lemon juice. Stir well and taste. If necessary adjust the flavour by adding more lemon juice or, if necessary, sweeten with a little icing sugar.

4. Freeze in an ice cream maker, following the manufacturer's instructions. If you do not have one, pour the mixture into a metal or plastic freezer container and freeze for about 2-3 hours or until set. Turn it out, chop roughly into 7cm/3in pieces, then whizz in a food processor until smooth. Return to the freezer container and freeze again until firm. Repeat this freezing-chopping process 2 or 3 times until a smooth sorbet consistency is reached.

Come the Autumn, there is a multitude of fruits and berries to gather from the countryside; so armed with baskets I set out for a day's leisurely picking. Elderberries I have already mentioned (see recipe), everyone knows how to use blackberries; but what of rosehips? They can be infused for a syrup or boiled for about two hours, then strained, sweetened with sugar, thickened with a tablespoon of potato flour and flavoured with almonds for a delicate sweet soup.

Haws – hawthorn berries – transform into a delicate pink jelly although perhaps my favourite comes from rowan berries boiled up with apples and sugar; it is delightful served with roast venison. Sloes can be pricked all over with a needle, covered with gin and left to stand, stoppered in a bottle, until Christmas when the sloe gin is ready to drink. Crab apples can be cooked up into a wine, jelly or, perhaps more unusually, a 'cheese' – which is actually an old-fashioned method of making a thick jam using plenty of sugar but only a little water flavoured with cloves, cinnamon or ginger.

If you do go out into the countryside, remember not to stray onto private land.

Plum Crumble
With Cinnamon Custard

*The Victoria plum we all seem to know; but have you ever tasted a
'Warwickshire Droper' or 'Coe's Golden Drop' or 'Pershore' (Yellow Egg)?
Sadly we seem to be concentrating on growing just a few well-known varieties
throughout the country. As a result we risk losing the richness and glories of
regional variations. Serves 6–8.*

1.35kg/3lbs plums
30-85g/1-3oz caster sugar

Crumble
55g/2oz chopped walnuts
115g/4oz granulated sugar
85g/3oz plain flour
85g/3oz butter, diced

Custard
4 egg yolks
55g/2oz home-made vanilla
  sugar (see page 76)
575ml/1pt milk
½tsp ground cinnamon

1. Preheat the oven to 190°C/375°F/gas mark 5.

2. Halve and stone the plums. Arrange them in a shallow baking dish and sprinkle
   with sugar. How much you use will depend on how ripe and sweet are the
   plums.

3. To make the crumble, mix the walnuts, sugar and flour together. Rub in the
   butter with your fingertips until you have a crumbly texture and spread evenly
   over the plums. Bake in the preheated oven for about 35 minutes or until the
   fruit is tender. If the crumble starts to brown too quickly, cover lightly with foil.

4. Meanwhile make the custard. Whisk the egg yolks with the sugar until they
   thicken. In a heavy-based saucepan bring the milk to a boil, then whisk half of
   the hot milk into the egg yolks and return this egg mixture back into the
   remaining milk, whisking continuously. Cook over very low heat – a heat
   diffuser is really useful here – stirring with a wooden spoon until the custard
   thickens slightly. Then remove from the heat and add the cinnamon. Serve with
   the crumble.

PLUMS BAKED IN SAUTERNES

A stunning but simple recipe that comes from Nigel Slater's Real Fast Puddings. You can use any variety of plum you like although for the best possible flavour, he recommends greengages. Serves 2–4.

30g/1oz butter
85g/3oz caster sugar
12 medium plums

125ml/4fl oz Sauternes
or any sweet wine
cream, to serve

1. Pre-heat the oven to 200°C/400°F/gas mark 6.

2. Rub the butter around the inside of a shallow baking dish and sprinkle in the sugar.

3. Halve and stone the plums. Arrange them in the dish and bake for about 10 minutes in the preheated oven.

4. Remove from the oven and baste the plums with any juices in the bottom of the dish. Then pour in the wine, return to the oven and bake for a further 15-20 minutes or until the plums are tender and the cooking juices bubbling. This will depend on the ripeness of the plums.

5. Serve with the buttery juices spooned over the plums and plenty of cream.

FLOWERPOT CHIVE BREAD

Bread baked in individual flowerpots looks very appealing, particularly if you serve the loaves in the pots arranged on the table. The idea comes from Richard Cawley's book Appetizing Outdoor Eating.
Makes 8 miniature loaves.

1tbsp olive oil, plus extra for greasing
675g/1½lb strong white flour, plus extra for dusting

1sachet/1tbsp 'fast-action' yeast
1½tsp salt
450ml/¾pt hand-hot water
6tbsp chopped chives

1. Well ahead of time, wash thoroughly 8 new terracotta flower pots, each measuring about 8cm/3in across the top and 8cm/3in high. Allow them to dry well.

2. Preheat the oven to 200°C/400°F/gas mark 6.

3. Brush the inside of the flower pots with oil, then dust them thoroughly with flour, tipping out any excess. Line the bottoms with circles of greaseproof paper.

4. Put the flour in a large bowl with the yeast and salt. Stir in the oil and hot water and bring the mixture together to form a ball of dough. Knead for a good 10 minutes, working in the chives for the last 1-2 minutes.

5. Divide the dough into 8 equal portions. Roll each one into an elongated ball shape and put in one of the prepared flower pots. Cover and leave in a warm place for 1-2 hours, until the dough has risen over the top of the flower pots.

6. Bake for 20-25 minutes. When cooked the loaves should sound hollow if tapped on the bottom. Run a knife around the top edge of each of the loaves to loosen and then turn out of the pot. Peel off the circles of greaseproof paper and allow the loaves to cool.

7. Serve the loaves in their flower pots.

ROSEMARY FOCACCIA

Focaccia has a crumbly almost cake-like texture; you can make it with fresh sage,
thyme, or a mixture of all the herbs too. It never fails to please.

25g/1oz fresh cake yeast
or 15g/½oz active dry yeast
a pinch of sugar
1tsp salt
350g-400g/12-14oz strong

or plain flour
3tbsp olive oil
2 sprigs of fresh rosemary,
coarse stalks removed
coarse sea salt

1. Warm a medium mixing bowl by swirling some hot water in it and drain. Put in the yeast and pour over 250ml/8fl oz lukewarm water. Stir in the sugar, mix together and allow to stand for 5-10 minutes or until the yeast starts to foam.

2. Using a wooden spoon, stir in the salt and about one third of the flour. Then mix in another third of the flour, stirring with the spoon until the dough forms a mass and begins to pull away from the sides of the bowl.

3. Sprinkle some remaining flour onto a smooth work surface. Place the dough on top and start to knead it, working in the remaining flour a little at a time, until all is incorporated. Knead for 8-10 minutes until the dough is elastic and smooth; form into a ball.

4. Lightly oil a mixing bowl. Place the dough in the bowl and cover with a damp towel. Leave to stand in a warm place for about 45-50 minutes or until the dough has doubled in volume. Poke two fingers into the dough; if the indentations remain, the dough is ready.

5. Preheat the oven to 200°C/400°F/gas mark 6.

6. Punch the dough down with your fist and knead for 3-4 minutes. Brush a large shallow baking pan with about 1 tablespoon of the oil. Place the dough in the pan and press it into an even layer about 2cm/1in thick. Scatter with the rosemary leaves, cover the dough and leave to rise in a warm place for 30 minutes.

7. Just before baking use your fingers to press row of light indentations into the surface of the focaccia. Brush with the remaining 2 tablespoons of oil and sprinkle lightly with coarse sea salt. Bake for about 25 minutes or until just golden. Cut into squares and serve warm.

JAMS AND PRESERVES

Onion Marmalade

Serve an onion marmalade with a pâté, cold meats or sausages. If you like a contrast of textures, try making it with a mixture of onions, shallots and even a few white pearl onions. Makes 4 x 300ml/½pt jars.

3tbsp extra virgin olive oil
900g/2lb onions, sliced
5 shallots, sliced
85g/3oz light muscovado sugar
salt and freshly ground
  black pepper

4tbsp honey
300ml/½pt red wine
75ml/5tbsp cider vinegar
a handful of raisins

1. Heat the olive oil in a large frying pan, stir in the onions, shallots and sugar. Season with salt and pepper. Cover the pan and cook over a gentle heat for 30 minutes, stirring occasionally with a wooden spoon.

2. Add the honey, wine, vinegar and raisins. Carry on cooking over very low heat, still stirring from time to time for about 20 minutes or until the onions make a thick syrup.

3. Remove from the heat immediately and pour into hot sterilized jars. Seal in the usual way and leave to stand for at least 2-3 weeks before even trying it. Once you have opened the jar, keep it cool in the refrigerator.

No kitchen should ever be without onions and the best of all onions for cooking are fat and juicy, white or pale-cream fleshed and for ease of cutting, globe shaped. Red onions have a hazily sweet taste and an arresting beetroot-red skin; I prefer them raw, chopped or sliced into rings in salsas (see page 44) or salads although they can be roasted successfully if lightly brushed with olive oil.

Another useful member of the onion family is the baby white pearl; it performs splendidly in stews and soups as it holds together well, imparting only the mildest of flavours. Pickling onions – when still young – can be successfully substituted but the older ones tend to an overpowering harshness. Spring onions are mildly flavoured – use them raw or when you want to cook really fast; after being subjected to a few minutes heat, their flavour disappears. Welsh onions may look like a spring onion, but have a stronger, sharper bite.

Shallots are thought to be far more gently flavoured but it does depend on the variety – the grey-brown skinned ones can be tremendously pungent. Whatever onions you use, make sure they are firm to touch, unblemished and quite dry.

FLAVOURED SUGARS

Most cooks know about vanilla sugar, made by packing a vanilla pod in a jar of plain white sugar and leaving it to scent and flavour the sugar, but certain herbs, leaves or flowers work equally well. Use them sprinkled over fruit or add them to tarts, ice creams, sorbets or pies; try Rosemary Sugar sprinkled over strawberries, or Pelargonium Sugar with apples or plums. My favourites are a few well chosen leaves from Pelargonium Tomentosum with its sharp mint aroma or 'Lemon Fancy' with its citrus appeal. Lavender Sugar is glorious with gooseberries and Rose Sugar transforms a milk pudding.

To make a scented sugar, chose your herbs, leaves or flowers carefully, avoiding any that are bruised or blemished or overblown. Wash or wipe them with a damp cloth and pat dry. Then take a well-washed preserving jar with a tight fitting lid and pour in a little sugar – either caster or granulated will do. Then add a layer of your chosen herb, leaf or flower, add a little more sugar and carry on until the jar is packed full. Close it tightly and leave to stand for at least three weeks so the flavours infuse. And the first time you open the jar, you will enchanted with the scent.

SWEET SOUR CHERRIES

An Elizabeth David recipe from *French Provincial Cooking*. Although Miss David thinks these cherries are not a typical French recipe, she first came across them served like olives in Châteauneuf du Pape, as part of a mixed hors d'oeuvre. And they are obviously a useful standby, for they will keep for a year.

"For each pound (450g) of morello cherries (the bright bitter red cherries which come into season in August) use 6oz (170g) of white sugar, 12fl oz (350ml) of wine vinegar and 6 whole cloves. Leave an inch or so of stalk on the cherries, discard any that are at all damaged or bruised, and pack the rest into wide preserving jars, filling them three quarters full.

Boil the vinegar, sugar and cloves together for 10 minutes. Leave until cold and then pour over the cherries. Screw down the tops and leave a month before opening."

FLAVOURED VINEGARS

The uses of flavoured vinegars are too numerous to recount. Use them in stews, salads, soups, marinades, dressings or sauces. Like flavoured sugars, the basic principle is to steep herbs, flowers, fruits or vegetables in vinegar so they are infused with flavour.

Use only a proper vinegar – white or red wine or cider. Never even think of trying a malt vinegar or a non-brewed condiment. Fill a bottle with about one-third of the flavouring to two-thirds vinegar, then leave it, tightly stoppered, for at least a couple of weeks before you think of sampling it. Some people prefer to strain it before use, others are quite happy to leave the vinegar with the flavourings in – it is up to you.

Some suggestions for flavourings are raspberries, blackberries, black currants, loganberries, mulberries or elderberries. Interesting herbs and flowers are rosemary, sage, tarragon, thyme or thyme flowers or elderflowers. Shallots, garlic or even cucumbers make excellent flavoured vinegars.

All you do is wash and pat dry the flavourings, strip the fruit and flowers off their stems, peel and slice – in the case of cucumbers – or peel and crush – in the case of garlic and shallots – the vegetables. Then pour in the vinegar. Do not worry if the proportions are not exact; just remember the more flavourings you put in, the stronger the taste will be.

ROAST RASBERRY JAM

Everyone has their favourite way of making jams. To the countless recipes I wish to add this foolproof method of making raspberry jam – it never fails. Equally importantly it makes the most intense tasting, fruity jam I have ever come across.

All you do is to take equal quantities of raspberries – the riper the better – and sugar. Put these in a medium oven 190°C/375°F/gas mark 5 for about 20 minutes until the fruit has softened. Then, using a wooden spoon, you break the fruit down to a purée and bottle it. You can, if you like your jams with added flavour, add a little gently heated vodka or a few chopped lemon balm leaves or even a dash of lemon. Otherwise just leave it perfectly plain, bottle it and eat away to your heart's content.

GENERAL INDEX